Photography Lighting

Top 10 Must-Know Photography Lighting Facts to Shoot Like a Pro in Your Home Studio

James Carren

For more books by this author, please visit
www.photographybooks.us

Table of Contents

Table of Contents

Introduction
So You Want a Studio

Working as a photographer is a hard and highly costly business. Since the advent of the digital era, many people think that photography is free, and so they expect low rates for a lot of work. We as photographers know that this is a myth, and at best, only a half-truth. While it does cost nothing to deliver solely digital images, it takes time and effort to make them, and a significant amount of money to afford all of the necessary equipment for a studio. Because of this, a lot of photographers choose to rent equipment and space from other places, either via hourly, daily, or weekly rates.

While this can be an excellent solution to begin with, depending on the availability of someone else's things can be tiresome. If this sounds like you, or you think that your business is about to become especially prolific, you may want to consider setting up your own home studio. This can be a practical choice at any level—whether student or professional—although you will have to be willing to invest a fair amount of money over a period of time that is convenient for you.

In this book, I will start off talking about the advantages and disadvantages of having a home studio, ways to determine the cost of your home studio, and different levels of what it means to have a home studio. In other words, I want to teach you the difference between a very basic home studio and a fully-equipped one. Moving on from start-up costs and levels of affordability, I'll discuss what industry standard lighting equipment is and some of the options that are available to you. Finally, I will introduce various lighting set-ups, requiring various numbers of lights, additional tools (such as softboxes), and unique arrangements.

Though you will, of course, need to do your own research to determine exact pricing and to figure out what you want in your studio, I hope that this book can be a comprehensive beginner's tool for you to turn to as you set up your studio, as well as a guide as you advance your lighting skills.

Chapter 1
Finding a Space

If you've worked in a studio before (which you probably have), you know that before you can go ahead with anything else, you have to find a space. Optimally, you want this space to have wide, north-facing windows and a wall opposite those windows. This is the very minimum that you need. You also need to have plenty of room to move around in the space, enough for both photographer and model. Ideally, you will also want the walls of the room to be painted a solid, neutral color. Another option is to have all the walls painted a different color, allowing for versatility.

Alternatively, if you don't have access to a room with north-facing windows, any room with big windows and a facing wall will do. Or, if you have no interest in accessing natural light, you can make use of a room that has no windows. This would be my last choice though, because it's always better to have more options than not enough, and you can always cover the windows with heavy, black, light-blocking curtains if you want to fully control the light.

So how much space should you have to move around in? Well, you don't want to be too close to your model, especially if you want the freedom of backing up and getting closer for different angles. I would suggest no less than fifteen feet of moving space, although you should try to find more if you can. If you only have one room in your home for your studio, select the biggest one that's available to you.

Also, be observant. What features does a room have that might make it a perfect fit for a studio? For example, does any room in your house feature sliding doors that separate it from another room? If so, these two adjoining rooms are probably perfect, because you have the option of shutting the door for a smaller studio or opening them up to expand your space for larger shoots.

The other consideration you have to make when it comes to home studios is furniture. While every studio should have some furniture for you, the models, and your assistants, how much is too much? One of the problems I run into is that the perfect space is also part of your living area, and so you have to constantly rearrange the furniture. If this is the case, you really have two options: either you can live with it, and put those non-scratch, sticky pads on the bottoms of table and chair legs to protect your floors, or you can do a little feng shui and consolidate your furniture. I would honestly suggest the latter, unless you have a convenient space that you can scoot all unwanted furniture into during shoots. It all comes down to priority, and whether you entertain more than you shoot, or vice versa. You may even find that rearranging gives you the space and room to breathe, and if you have to sell some of your furniture, well, that's more money for equipment.

Finally, it's great if your room has a small closet for storing your studio essentials, so that they don't crowd up the space during shoots.

Chapter 2
Basic Equipment—
Backdrops, Stands, and Lights

So what basic equipment do you need in a studio? Assuming you've done studio work before, you know the equipment you tend to use the most. Because most people don't have thousands of dollars to drop on equipment, however, start with the very minimum and work your way up from there.

Here is my list of basic equipment. Feel free to add or take away from it as you see fit; this is only a starting point to consider.

Backdrops

Even if you have a nice, plain wall to work with, sometimes you might want to switch things up a bit, or you may need to easily remove a subject from its background. In situations like these, you'll want a backdrop, also referred to as a seamless. In fact, you'll probably want a variety of them. At the outset, I would suggest at least four: one full and one half black seamless, and one full and one half white seamless.

I mostly shop at B&H Photo and Video for the majority of my photographic supplies. Their things are always professional industry standard and tend to be the most affordable for their quality. Most of their seamless papers run 107 inches by 12 yards, which is around $46 before tax, or 53 inches by 12 yards, which is around $25 before tax. There are also other options—some come as long as 50 yards—so it all depends on your needs.

To use seamless paper, roll out what you need for the backdrop and some for the floor as well (unless you're just doing headshots, in which case you only need enough paper to cover about from head to shoulder height). The paper on the floor will get stepped on by the model, meaning that unless she is barefoot, you will need to cut off that length of paper after the shoot. Don't worry, though. A large seamless should last you a good while.

The first measurement, in inches, denotes how wide the paper is, so if you have a specific area you would like to cover, I would measure that space before ordering. Although white seamless paper is very versatile because you can change its look easily in Photoshop, I would also recommend a neutral grey, which looks really good for portraits. And if you don't want to do all of your work in Photoshop, invest in other seamless papers; they are available in every color imaginable, and as you figure out your tendencies, you can decide what colors you need the most.

Aside from seamless papers, there are other types of backdrops you can use for a more dramatic effect. These include cloth backdrops, such as those made out of cotton, muslin or velvet. Unless you run a children's studio, or make a lot of conceptual art, I would suggest generally veering away from these types of things. This category also includes hand painted backdrops, which can look very cheesy. Nonetheless, they are an option if you want them, and they can provide interesting background texture for certain types of work.

Aside from removable backdrops, you may also want to think about permanent ones, which Of course can be covered by a seamless or cloth if need be. By this I mean, if your chosen room has any cool textures, such as wood or exposed brick or interesting paint layers, don't remove them. This kind of thing gives a place dimension and character, and you might be surprised how many clients request a backdrop of this kind.

If you're bummed because your studio hasn't got anything like that, no worries. You can make these kinds of backdrops out of pieces of wood, stone, or even foam core painted to look like the texture you want. Just make sure you commission a talented artist to create these kinds of trompe l'oeil pieces for you.

Stands

You can't very well put up a seamless without stands, and the most common type is referred to as the C-stand. The C-stand is very heavy and durable, as it is made from metal. They are harder to store than their lighter fiberglass or plastic counterparts, so while they can be expensive, I would suggest investing in a few. They are great for holding up lights, and also, with a crossbar installed, great for your seamless to hang off of.

There are many adaptations you can make to the standard C-stand which will make it even more helpful. If you don't want to have to physically lug it around every time you need to shift a set-up during a shoot, you can get a rolling bottom for it.

If you plan on doing more theatrical lighting or even video, you might also want to invest in what is called a boom arm. Boom arms are extra attachments that go on top of C-stands, to which you then attach your lighting equipment, allowing it to hang down from above at a higher angle than what you could do without it.

The second most common type of lighting stand is called a tripod stand, so-called because it has three legs, but unlike C-stands, they aren't spaced the same. They tend to be lighter than C-stands.

With any light stand, you'll need sandbags to weight the legs so that they don't topple over, especially if the equipment is heavy or you're going to be having a lot of foot traffic around the set-up. Before you buy your stands, you need to think about which lights you'll be buying and how many, in order to determine the type and number of stands you will need.

Lights

Now comes the fun part and the meat of your studio. The lights. There are so many types of lights that will give you completely different looks. I will try to give a comprehensive overview of each type of light and what it does, as well as a general price range. There are two main lighting types that systems and lights can be divided into, and these are:

Continuous Lighting

Continuous lighting simply refers to light that doesn't flash. When thinking of in-studio photo shoots, people tend to think of strobe lighting, although as you'll see, this isn't always true. Continuous light refers not only to its non-flash qualities, but also to certain types of light bulbs. These include CFL light bulbs, LED lights, HMIs, and tungsten lights. As previously stated, all of these will emit constant light. As you will see, some of the types have some overlap, because the title refers to more specialized lights of the same family.

Tungsten, or Hot Lights

Let's start with the tungsten light, since, as you will see, it is the most familiar type. Tungsten lights are also commonly referred to as hot lights, and this is what I find myself using most often, mostly because they are readily available. Hot lights often come equipped with their own modifiers, usually in the form of a rounded reflector shade. Tungsten light is warm in color, and this is why there is a tungsten white balance setting on your camera. Make sure you use this to avoid overly warm color shifts.

There are a few glaring (pardon the pun) problems with hot lights. They are called hot lights because they tend to use a lot of energy and thus get very hot very quickly. Therefore, if you're planning a long shoot, you wouldn't want to use hot lights for a variety of reasons. And it you were to fit it with any light modifier other than the reflector it comes with—particularly a cloth one—it might actually get too hot and catch fire. Not only that, but hot lights can be bad for portraiture, since they will make your subject sweat much quicker than other lights, due to the heat.

The only real advantage to tungsten lights (other than their color, if that's what you're after) is that they are cheap, and this, unfortunately, is why I end up using them if I don't have access to anything else. However, they also give you a more accurate representation the light that's going to be in your final image, whereas strobe setups and other continuous lights can require more guesswork and getting used to.

Tungsten lights may also be referred to as halogen lights, or vice versa.

Fluorescent/CFL Lightbulbs

Fluorescent lights can be mounted either on a panel or they can be what is called a CFL: a compact fluorescent lightbulb. In contrast to tungsten lights, fluorescent lights use much less power and do not pose a risk of fire or injury. They also will not overheat your model as fast, so they are better for portraiture, as opposed to tungsten lights, which are better for product photography and still-life photos.

The downside to using fluorescent light is that it can appear a lot harsher and less flattering than tungsten. It can also wash your subject out if you aren't careful with the set-up and don't use modifiers. On the upside, though, fluorescent lights are much safer to use with modifiers, so you can make the light quality more pleasing with a little work.

Because they use less power than the tungsten light, it is also possible that, depending on what you're lighting, you'll need to use more lights than you would when using tungsten.

LED Panels

LED panels are, to my knowledge, the newest to the lighting industry when it comes to continuous light sources. LEDs not only come in panel format, but also as spots and floods, although the panels do seem more common. Like HMI and tungsten lights, LEDs can be daylight balanced, which means they are still as warm as tungsten lights but without the weird color casts. They also have the advantages of fluorescents in that they require very little energy to run. Unlike a lot of other continuous lights, they can be color balanced as needed for warm or cool tones.

HMI Lights

HMI lights are also known by various other names, but are standard in the film industry. Like traditional tungsten lights, they give off a lot of heat and power, which, until recently, required frequent bulb replacement. Like LED, they can be daylight balanced. I would not consider this type of light as a viable option for any startup studio, due to the cost and frequent replacement needs.

So there's your run down of continuous light sources, what they look like, and how they work. Next, before continuing on to flash or strobe Lighting, I want to talk about price points, and what, in the continuous lighting arena, I would consider good for a start-up home studio.

Though some full lighting kits that feature tungsten can be as expensive as one HMI light, you end up with much more product for your money. In fact, some starter reflector floodlights only run from about $24-48. Of course, that is not to say that they can't get expensive too. For example, if you purchase a high-end tungsten Fresnel, by Arri, you may wind up paying close to $400.

The cost of professional fluorescent lights is much the same, and except in a pinch, I really wouldn't suggest using the fluorescent bulbs already present in your house. Professional lights, again, will cost a little over $100.

LED lights are slightly more expensive than tungsten or fluorescent, in the middle price point. They tend to run between $200 and $500.

Finally, there is HMI, which runs into the thousands if not tens of thousands of dollars.

Search around and decide what type or brand of light you feel best suits you. Start out with tungsten and fluorescent, and if you find yourself really liking the tungsten, maybe try an Arri Fresnel. Keep in mind that there are so many brands and styles of these lights on the market, so do your research and price comparisons, determine what lighting set-ups you find the most pleasing, and purchase accordingly. The good news is that if you end up not liking a light, you will always be able to sell it, as long as it's in good shape, but I would try to avoid that route, as you don't want to irresponsibly lose money on such expensive gear.

Flash or Strobe Lighting

The other type of studio lighting relies on flash, and is what people readily think of when they envision professional studio lighting. Strobe lighting can be divided into two different types: power packs and monolights. When I do use a flash in-studio, I tend to use power packs.

Electronic Flash/Power Packs

Electronic flash means that the power of the flash is generated and controlled by a power pack. The kind of power pack I'm familiar with is called a Pocket Wizard, although there are other brands. You connect your head, or light, to the power pack via a jack, and adjust all of your settings accordingly. This way, every time you fire your shutter, the power pack responds by causing the light to emit a flash for whatever length of time you have specified.

The packs that I'm familiar with, that correspond with the Pocket Wizard, are made by Profoto. As many have found, these packs can be a bit confusing, especially if you have been trained with monolights, which I will explain in the following section. On some Profoto packs, you can connect multiple lights, which is of course, excellent if you have a multiple light set-up, although it can easily be used with a single light as well.

Let's say you choose to hook up all three connections. Each one will have its own corresponding letter, be it A, B, or A+B. For each head, you will tell the pack whether you want the light at full power, half power, or quarter power. With the Pocket Wizard, you can test the lights to make sure your exposure is correct, but be very careful not to blind yourself. Often, even with one light, you won't want to put it on full power.

Going into everything about the power pack would require its own book, so if you are unfamiliar and decide to invest in one, take the time to read the manual and familiarize yourself with the pack and Pocket Wizard.

Monolights

These function with the same purpose as power packs, but are a lot simpler to learn on and figure out. This is because everything is located on the light itself. You don't have a separate power pack, so you can just plug your light in, set it up on a stand, and go. All the settings are present on the light itself, making it easy to control.

Chapter 3
All About Modifiers, Plus Interesting Ways to Create Shadow

You may think that now that you've got your backdrop, stands and lights, you're ready to go. You're almost there, but not quite. My favorite part of studio lighting is the modifiers. Modifiers allow you to more fully direct the light you're using. With modifiers, you can make light softer, harsher, more concentrated, or more diffused. You can bounce it toward the subject to create highlights, or you can deflect it to control your shadows and the way they fall. You can affect the temperature and the look of your highlights and shadows or purposefully create and remove color casts as needed.

Umbrella

Let's start out with the most common light modifier that people think of. This is the umbrella. Umbrellas can come in either black or white, and both do different things. Positioned above your light, white umbrellas allow the light to completely envelop your model. Umbrellas also help to produce much softer, diffused light, as a soft box does, but with less restraint. Due to the curved nature of the umbrella, the light will spill out along the sides, which will cause the it to bounce off all of the walls in the room. Umbrellas are excellent to start with due to the fact that they are cheap, light, and don't require much exactness to work well.

Black umbrellas, unlike their white counterparts, are used sort of like reflectors to brighten or throw highlights onto a subject. The silver (or other colored metallic inside of the umbrella) serves as the reflector, while the black directs the light inward to the reflector.

Reflectors

Since I've mentioned reflectors so much already, I figured that should be the next section. Be aware that, aside from umbrella reflectors, there are also metal reflectors (that function and look sort of like lampshades) and handheld reflectors. The lampshade reflectors often come with a basic lighting kit, and are fixed directly over the light, instead of in front or above like an umbrella is. Tilted down on the subject, the light will strike the silver metal interior and reflect on the subject, typically to provide more light on the face.

Handheld reflectors are much more versatile, and can often be used in conjunction with other lighting reflectors that are directly on the lights. These kinds of reflectors can be angled onto a subject's face or any other portion of the body that needs to be highlighted, either by an assistant or by a boom arm (if it needs to be placed very high).

Handheld reflectors come in all sorts of colors, and I have found that the most economical way to make sure you have everything you need is to get an all-in-one reflector. For example, I have a six-in-one reflector, which can be flipped and zipped, inside and out, so you can access all of the colors it provides. It comes with: a white reflector, a black diffuser (which helps direct light away from the subject), and silver, gold, bronze, and rosy pink metallic reflectors. This way, you can pop whatever kind or tone of highlight you need onto wherever you need it with much more precision than an umbrella.

Diffusers and reflectors may also be referred to as flags, and they are the same, except that flags are often larger and come on poles for easier handling.

Soft Box

Personally, my favorite kind of modifier is a soft box. Soft boxes are like large square or rectangular tents that can be fitted via a speed ring onto a bare light. A soft box is actually made up of two zippered pieces, an inner reflective piece and an outer diffuser. If you leave the outer diffuser on, you're going to create very soft, even, controlled light that is awesome for instantly flattering portraits. If you take the outer diffuser off, you'll get a much harsher light, just as if you were shooting with a very large reflector.

Soft boxes also come in a huge variety of sizes, and you'll want to select a size based on the area you plan to cover. For most normal, small, one- or two-client shoots, one small or medium soft box will work just fine.

Other Types of Soft Boxes

These include strip lighting and an octagon shaped soft box called an octabox. I like to think of octaboxes as giant love children, with the benefits of both a soft box and an umbrella. Like a soft box, octaboxes come in all different sizes, and like a soft box, the bigger the octabox, the softer and more diffused the light is.

Strip lighting is, again, basically the same as a soft box, except that it comes in varying lengths and is shaped more like a rectangle than a square. It's optimal for side lighting due to the nature of its shape, but also remember that due to its shape, it isn't optimal for much else because the beam is so narrow.

Beauty Dish

While the beauty dish is also a light diffuser, its shape provides a much harsher, concentrated beam of light. With another diffuser, or sock, placed over it, the light becomes softer than it would be without, but still retains some of that harsh quality. The beauty dish is so-called because it was often used in old beauty advertisements to make features such as the eyes and cheekbones more pronounced. It's also incredibly dramatic lighting, and while it may look great on a supermodel or a male, it won't look great on someone who doesn't already have strong features.

Barn Doors

Barn doors look and function exactly how they sound and can be especially convenient for directing light: determining where it goes and where it doesn't. Use them for backdrops or to create dramatic shadows on the face of a model for experimental lighting purposes.

Snoot

A snoot is like a tiny funnel which serves to direct a tiny concentrated beam of light onto a subject. It can be used to achieve separation between an object and its background, or to light up a small detail on a product, such as a delicate piece of jewelry.

Gels

Gels are color filters for your lights. Unlike the above modifiers, they do not shape or otherwise direct light, they simply help to control the mood of the shoot. While you can get filters that will fit directly over a light, you don't have to. The easiest way to go about using gels is to clamp them onto a light, and when you shoot the picture, the light will filter through the gel to create the desired color. While it may not look like it has much effect in person, you'll see that in camera, it does do a lot to change the mood of the shot.

Creative Ways to Modify Light and Play With Shadow

Part of the fun of working in the studio with all these lights and modifiers is to experiment. I saw a beautiful series done by a colleague once, in which she used various household objects and knickknacks to create intriguing shadows on her models. She did this by holding the objects up in front of the model, as close as she could get without actually being in the photo, and allowed the light to shine through them, creating harsh lines and forms and patterns.

You can create such shadows—if you want to experiment—by using any common, household appliance you can think of. Some will work out better than others, and it will take some trial and error, but if you take your time and have fun with it, you may end up with something really cool.

Chapter 4
Props and Other Materials to Keep Around the Studio

Now that all the essentials have been taken care of, let's talk about other miscellaneous things that are good to have around the studio at all times. There are different things you might need depending on whether you shoot still-life, commercial portraiture, or fine artwork, but one thing all photographers need is a toolbox.

In the toolbox, I would suggest having the usual suspects, such as hammers, nails, screwdrivers, tape, tape measure, pliers, glue, and a coin, just in case anything should need a quick fix. Also keep handy things you might find in a sewing box, especially safety pins, clothing tape, thread, and a few sizes of needles. This will keep you prepared for anything from a loose screw, to a too-tight tripod mount, to a ripped soft box cover, to a fashion emergency.

If you are a still-life photographer, it may be a good idea to keep some sawhorses and a plank or two of wood around, as well as fabrics of varying color and texture, should you ever need a makeshift table for a product shot. In this case, set up your backdrop and then arrange the wood plank on the sawhorses, creating a flat surface. Cover it if need be, and then set up your shot.

If you do a lot of product shots or you just want a really interesting look for your still-life photos, I would also suggest investing in about two pieces of plexiglass, one white and one black. You can either have it cut flat, or cut with what is referred to as an "infinity cut," meaning that the piece of plexi can serve both as backdrop and tabletop surface.

For a portrait photographer, it's going to be very important that you have various seating arrangements for clients, both for while they wait and to be used within the shoots. You'll want to have varying stools, chairs, and even crates because you never know what kind of seating arrangement would best suit the height or comfort of a particular client. To add a touch of whimsy, especially if you shoot a lot of children or family portraiture, you might also want to consider things like rocking chairs, beanbag chairs, or maybe even a hanging swing.

For family and beauty photography, you might also want to have a box of props around. Things like toys for small children, dog and cat stuffed animals, and glamorous accessories, such as gloves and costume jewelry.

And as always, every good studio photographer should have plenty of clamps around, for things like securing seamless paper, curtains, and gels.

Chapter 5
Tethering

Before we talk further about the types of light and how to set them up, I want to mention one more piece of equipment you should consider having in your studio.

Even though we have become so dependent on laptops, for studio lighting it's always a good idea to have a full-sized monitor. Full-sized monitors are easier to look at during shoots, and because the picture is much larger than it would be on a laptop screen or camera display, you can easily spot mistakes, unwanted blurring, or awkward posing and correct it before you move from the shooting to the retouching process.

But have you ever wondered how you can get your photos to go straight from your camera to your computer as they're being shot? It's a process called tethering, where you attach the camera to the computer via a tether, or long cord, which processes the information straight from the camera to the desktop computer. In order to do this, you'll need your computer, tether, and a tethering system such as Capture One.

What software such as Capture One does is allow you to use Lightroom in order to view, delete or correct images the instant after they are taken. If you are taking the photos, though, you might want to consider asking an assistant to man the computer and watch for things you do and don't like. Capture One makes everything that much more efficient, because you won't end up looking at your photos and thinking, "Aw man, I would have gotten that shot if I had moved her just slightly to the left."

Capture One is also extremely useful for when you have to do a shoot for a client. The client can stand in the back near the monitor and supervise the shoot and the images immediately to let you know if they're getting what they want.

Chapter 6
Lighting Types and Terms

Before I go into Chapters 7 and 8 on explaining lighting setups, there are a few types of lighting and lighting terms you should know. This will help you to better understand the terminology. All of these lighting types can be utilized within the studio to achieve whatever look you desire.

Key Light and Rim Light

Key light refers to the main light in any lighting set-up. Even if you're only working with one light, it's still your key light. Key lights generally shine onto the subject.

The second light in the mix is called the rim light, or the hair light, so-called because it is often used to spatially separate your subject's hair from the backdrop of an image. It can also be used for other separations or to create depth.

Back Light

If you're working with just window light, back light can be really hard to control. Back light means the window is perfectly illuminated, but the subject is far too dark. This is why you never want to shoot directly in front of a window.

However, when applied correctly, back light can really help your image. For example, if you back light your backdrop, and also have a key light on the subject, it can create some really nice drama and fill.

Side Light

Side light is very dramatic and is exactly what it sounds like: you light things from the side. This can create very dramatic shadows and a lot of chiaroscuro. Side light can also be harsh and very high contrast, so use it wisely.

Fill Light

Fill light, or ambient light, is often taken for granted and not utilized enough. This can be natural light, as it comes in through a window, or light that has been spread out and softened by modifiers, such as large soft boxes and octaboxes.

Chapter 7
Portraiture Lighting

I want to start out this chapter by stating that, in this and the following chapter, there is no possible way that I can cover every lighting set-up imaginable. My goal here is to provide you with lighting set-ups that will help you get started, and you can research and learn variations from there. Some of these lighting set-ups will require only one or two lights and some modifiers, which is fantastic for a start-up home studio and because of budget restrictions.

Two-Light Set-Up for a Basic Portrait

For this lighting set-up, you only need two lights, your main light, and your hair light, which will help to separate your subject from your backdrop. Put the hair light behind the model and adjust the height so it's just above his or her head, illuminating his or her hair. If you find that the light is too harsh around the head, use an appropriate light modifier, such as a soft box or even an umbrella, although a modifier may be more necessary on your key light. The key light (main light) is going to go just to one side of the camera, pointing at the subject, with a five-foot length of space between your model and the light.

Split Lighting

If you shoot a lot of male models, or you're looking for a lighting setup that will provide highly contrasted, dramatic light, then split lighting is for you. Similar to Rembrandt lighting, it allows part of the subject to be in shadow and part of the subject to emerge out of it.

For this arrangement, you only need one light source, which you will place at a 90 degree angle to your subject. If needed, place the light behind their head. Adjust and make sure that on the shadow side, their eye still catches the light. Split lighting is meant to shadow half of the face, but you don't want to completely obscure it or it will just look strange.

Also, the closer the light, the harsher the shadow, so play around with distance and with your soft boxes to see what level you would like. Remember that if you are working with continuous light, you'll get a much better idea of what the final product is going to look like than with strobe lighting. Keep in mind that men's faces are generally more suited to split lighting, because stronger bone structure holds up better in harsh, high-contrast light.

Loop Lighting

Loop lighting also utilizes one light, plus a reflector to bounce light back onto your subject. Loop lighting is recognizable by the tiny shadow it causes the nose to make on the cheek. Do not confuse it with butterfly lighting, which causes small shadows beneath the nose.

To create loop lighting, place your light source behind your subject, higher than their eye level. Play around with this a bit to make sure that the shadow is falling properly. Place a reflector, or have an assistant hold a reflector to the left of the camera, and angle it at the subject to bounce the light and create the proper shadow. Keep it at about mid-height to start, and go higher if need be, but never, ever start low and angle up. This isn't a good type of shadow to create, and it isn't very flattering either.

Butterfly Lighting

Butterfly lighting, like loop lighting, creates a shadow on the face under the nose. It is called butterfly lighting because the shape the shadows make is reminiscent of a butterfly. Butterfly lighting is very flattering, since it makes cheekbones appear higher. It used to be used a lot in the beauty industry, along with the help of a beauty dish, I'm sure. Interestingly, I have heard it said by some people that this light is too harsh for women and is commonly used on men. While you can of course use this and any lighting set-up with a male, I maintain that it is very flattering on women. Also, use it on models with weak bone structure, as it will flatter the features they do have.

Take one light and set it up about five feet from the model, placing your light directly in front of the model. You'll want it raised up a few feet above their head, so there isn't any one height I can give; it depends on the model. Angle the light down on the model. This will create the butterfly shadow. If you want that shadow to be stronger, dial up the strength of your light and try a few shots. Alternately, if you still want the look of the light but want it to be more diffused, try it with any variation of the soft box. It could also be interesting to see a beauty dish used in conjunction with this set-up.

One Light

Have you ever only had one light to work with, tried to work with it, and then gotten frustrated and given up because it just looked too harsh? Well let me explain to you how to do it properly, although if you do have your own home studio, I trust you probably have more than one light. However, this can still be useful if you just need one quick shot for a project, or for when you have to do a very fast shoot. Also be aware that you can create lots of variations, even just with one light, by changing the distance between light and model, and by adding a soft box or other preferred modifier, or incorporating a reflector.

So, place your one light behind the subject, raised slightly above the head and tilted down at a forty-five degree angle. Remember that as always, this is just a guideline, and you may need to adjust the height, angle and distance to achieve the look you want.

Rembrandt

As dramatic and difficult as Rembrandt lighting may look, it's really just as easy as anything else to do. Put the light behind your subjects at about a forty-five degree angle from them. Have them also angle their bodies slightly away from the light, in order to make sure that, as with split lighting, the shadow is partially obscuring one half of their faces. You also want the light to be up higher than your model's height.

The trick to knowing whether or not you're getting Rembrandt lighting correct is to check for the triangle of light that is going to fall down on your subject's nose and cheek. Also make sure the eye that is in shadow still has a catchlight in it, otherwise the set-up isn't correct and the end result will look odd.

Three-Point Lighting

A lot of people are daunted by the prospect of using more than two lights; I know I was when I first started in studio lighting. But you should remember that no matter how many lights you end up using in a shoot, you're just building up on configurations you already know how to do.

In the previous lighting set-ups I've mentioned, you typically make use of a key light and a rim light. In some, I've mentioned a key light and a background light. In order to get a three-point lighting set-up, you are going to be utilizing a key light, a fill light, and a background light. Though this is hard to explain without a diagram, there are plenty to be found online to assist you if you need it.

Here's how you do three-point lighting: Position your subject where you want him or her against your backdrop. Illuminate him or her with your key light. The brightness to which you set the key light depends on how bright you want the scene to be, but the latter also depends on the power output of all the lights. Generally, you want to start with your key light at max power.

Next, angle your fill light at the subject from his or her other side, probably at about a forty-five degree angle, but that depends upon the initial placement of the key light. This light is typically turned down to half power and may be softened via use of a soft box or beauty dish with a sock.

Finally, there's the background light, which you will shine directly onto the backdrop. Its power setting really just depends on how much illumination you want and what mood you're trying to create. Three-point lighting set-ups are often utilized with a strobe system instead of continuous lighting, although it can be done either way.

Clamshell Lighting

Clamshell lighting is so-called because when you set it up, it looks like the model is standing inside of a clamshell. The light also wraps around the model in such a way as you would think of being enveloped by standing in a clamshell.

In order to create the most flattering, least harsh light on your model, this is a setup where you might want to consider using two, if not three soft boxes. This way, the light will soften and spread. Remember to consider your options when it comes to the soft box style. While a regular, large or extra large soft box may be suitable for the background, consider using strip boxes instead of a traditional soft box for a different look.

The backdrop can either be lit by a separate light, or you can replace the backdrop altogether with a soft box in this case. No matter what modifiers you choose to use, the back light still remains the background light and should be at about half power in comparison to your key light, which should be the top front light.

Edge Lighting

Edge lighting is exactly what it sounds like; it puts emphasis on the edges and allows the rest of the photo to fall into dramatic shadow. This is the lighting you most often see in sports ads or very dramatic, high fashion editorials. I would suggest doing this shot on a darker background, because otherwise you'll need even more lights, which is fine too, it just all depends on what you have at your disposal and what you have time to set up.

With your dark background in place, set up lights with strip boxes on either side. These are your rim lights and in this case, they are the star of the show. They will also, for once, be cranked up to higher power than your key light, which should be at about half the power you select for your rim light.

As for your key light, it's going to be about two or three feet above the height of your model, so about seven or eight feet up, possibly on a boom arm for better angling.

Fashion Lighting

Forgive me the title of this section, because there are so many lighting set-ups that are used in fashion. This is just one of the many and actually doesn't involve a beauty dish. In fact, it's sort of like the feminine version of edge lighting. The rim lights are angled inward in much the same way as with edge lighting, but instead of using a beauty dish (with or without the grid) you're going to use a large soft box or octabox, angled down on the subject, although it doesn't have to be at quite the height of the beauty dish in the previous style.

I hope that this brief overview of portrait lighting has been helpful. Please do remember though, what I've been reiterating from the start of this book: lighting is so vast a skill that it can only be mastered through practice and experimentation. Be patient with yourself; using three lights in the studio really is the middle step to being good. Advanced lighting uses four or more lights, and should you choose to venture down that path, remember that those skills are simply building on what you already have learned from one-, two-, and three-light set-ups. If you are a beginner in studio lighting, start with the one- and two-light set-ups and slowly advance your way to four. If you're somewhat familiar with lighting and you feel confident and have the resources, step it up to three lights.

No matter what setups you choose to use, remember that as long as you're making the person in the photo look great, you're doing a good job.

Chapter 8
Still-Life Lighting

Believe it or not, still-life lighting works in much the same way as portrait lighting, just on a smaller scale and without worrying about the eyes. For example, if you're lighting flowers, you're still going to need a two-light setup, one backlight and one key light.

What's really cool is that, with still-life photos, depending on how large your objects are, you can use big lights or tiny desk lamp sized lights. Also, this is the area of photography where you really want to think about taking advantage of the snoot. The small, narrow beam of light is much more convenient for small details and will help to concentrate your light rather than letting it spread all over the place.

Also, still-life photography is where you're going to need all of those little odds and ends that I mentioned in Chapter 4: Sawhorses and planks or plexi function as great tables for you to arrange your objects on.

In fact, one of my favorite still-life lighting set-ups involves using plexi (either black or white, it doesn't matter) as the table and backdrop. So in this case, you would be using the infinity curved plexi. What you do is place a light on the floor underneath the plexi and it will shine up through the material, lighting your object from the bottom and making it appear to glow. For your second light, depending on preference, you can either point it at the background or you can shine it onto the objects. It really depends on your needs. I love experimenting with lighting from the bottom in still-life, since you rarely—if ever—have a chance to do so in portraiture.

Just as with portrait photography, the object of still-life is to hide imperfections and emphasize the good qualities. You never want to light an object straight on or with too much harsh flash, because it will blow out and look bad.

The good thing about still-life versus portraiture is that you can use a lot more dramatic and high-contrast light because you want to bring out as much detail as you can. Try using the same set-ups as you would with portraiture just to see what it'll do. With objects, you don't really have a generalized basis to go off of like you do with people, at least not until you get a feel for how similar shapes and textures react to different lighting conditions.

Some things to keep in mind about product photography are:

- You want to make sure the label and logo are in focus and sharp. Keep in mind though, that a lot of professional product photographers also keep digital versions of the labels and logos to make sure that it looks exactly as it should.

- They put the textures and colors on the products for a reason. With a professional product, such as, for example, Jose Cuervo tequila, they designed that bottle and selected that color palette specifically with the nature of their brand in mind. It's very important that you capture the correct colors and textures and don't alter it at all. Any discrepancy may require inordinate amounts of post production or even reshooting.

- Consider the mood of the brand when you choose how to light it. You know how to create smooth, flattering lighting, and very dramatic lighting from the section on lighting portraiture. What does the brand call for?

- Rim lighting can be used with a lot more freedom when it comes to still-life. Use it to highlight the edges of bottles or silver and really make it gleam.

- Sometimes it's hard to get as much drama or clarity as you want with very small objects such as delicate jewelry or silverware. Luckily, there are tent soft boxes that act as enclosed soft boxes. What you do is, place your item within the open space of the tent, and then enclose your camera lens in the ring of space that is there for it. This allows you to shoot straight into a fully surrounded soft box, which will provide a lot of very ambient, pleasing, even light.

- Keep in mind that in order to capture every single detail (this is especially applicable to product shots as opposed to artistic still-life, which is a lot more open-ended and less precise), you may have to take several shots that focus on different aspects or details of the item. You will then have to composite the images together to create the full product shot. You do not want to switch up the lighting at all during this process because you don't want to throw off any one shot because that will make the compositing process much harder.

- In order to learn how to light a still-life properly as well as creatively, I would suggest choosing an object that you enjoy and lighting it as many ways as you can think of.

Chapter 9
Keeping a Lighting Notebook

As you can probably tell from reading this ebook, lighting takes a lot of practice and a lot of trial-and-error. While I can give you some lighting set-ups to get started with, you have to understand that lighting is a continual learning process (as I have countlessly reiterated). Every principle that you learn with   basic lighting is similarly applied when you increase the number of lights involved. You are simply building on the same skills, and all of the lighting set-ups can be varied to involve five, six, or even seven lights. The choices you make are dependent upon your needs, the size of your space, and the size of your shoot.

Because lighting is so varied and complex, involving so many lights, modifiers, and settings as well as placements, I feel that it is extremely helpful to keep a lighting notebook. You do not have to section your lighting notebook by one light, two lights, three lights, et cetera, but I would suggest starting off your lighting notebook with the basic lighting setups you have learned here.

There are two ways that I can think to make the lighting notebook easy to navigate, and you should tab your notebook regardless of which route you choose. My first suggestion would be to color code it by the numbers of lights involved. However, this is sort of rudimentary and does not make as much sense as my next suggestion, which would be to color code your notebook by variation.

For example, if you have a bunch of lighting set-ups that are all very dramatic, group them together no matter how many lights each one of them has involved, because odds are the set-ups will be more similar to each other than with different groupings.

Let's talk about the organization of each page within your lighting notebook. If you know the name of the lighting setup, of course title it as such. But if your lighting setup is a variation or something you completely made up, you might want to title it something like variation of clamshell lighting using beauty dish or, if you have no reference points, dramatic lighting experiment using four lights just make sure the title will trigger your memory.

Directly underneath the title, I would put a list of all the lighting equipment down to the tiniest modifier that you have used. List what modifier was on what light, and across from this information put the amount of power you had going to each light. If you are also metering for your scene, include the overall exposure that you were happy with, even if you are shooting digital and have a record of it already.

If this is enough information for you, you can always stop there, but I would also recommend taking pictures of your lighting setup with the model in place for reference after you have achieved what you are looking for. Then, once you have tabbed everything according to your own organization system, using the book as a reference will be simple and save you a lot of headaches if you have to do a similar shoot weeks or months down the road.

Use whatever kind of notebook you prefer. It does not have to be a traditional bound paper notebook. You can keep these notes on your computer or tablet, just make sure they are backed up. If you do choose to go with a traditional notebook, you might want to store it with all of your other lighting equipment in a place where you can find it.

Conclusion

Though the world of studio lighting is vast, and I feel as though I have barely scratched the surface, I hope that this book was of some help to those of you getting started. The only real way to truly become a master at studio lighting is to play around with it. There are so many experimental possibilities that have not been discussed in these pages which will add truly daring and edgy looks to your photos.

If you have chosen to start your own, at-home studio, or even your own professional studio, you should now know the type of space you're looking for. Make sure you do your best to make this space as clear of distractions and other clutter as you can. This will help to ensure that your work flows smoothly and professionally and that it is organized.

Walking through the world of studio lighting equipment, you should now have a pretty good working understanding of the different types of light, the advantages and disadvantages of continuous and strobe lighting, and the differences between tungsten, fluorescent, LED, and HMI. Consider your needs and your price points when deciding what equipment to purchase, and always start with the things that will fulfill basic studio needs before investing in the very expensive and highly-specialized.

Do invest in all sorts of lighting modifiers, and figure out what other effects they can provide.

Use the basic, and even the more advanced lighting set-ups, as starting points for experimentation after you have mastered them. Keep a notebook full of these and other lighting set-ups you discover, full of sketches and notes on the equipment you used, as well as the settings of that equipment. A notebook is an invaluable resource that you can refer back to again and again if you get stuck or forget a detail. I find it to be a very important step in my understanding of lighting techniques, because you are already being inundated with so much new information and new technical skills needing to be mastered.

I cannot reiterate enough that lighting is a skill that must be practiced and experimented with; unlike knowledge of f/stops and shutter speeds, development times, and so many other elements of photography, you cannot memorize it all, because the needs of every shoot and every client will always be different.

Now that you've read this manual, sit down, make a spreadsheet, do your financial research, and make your purchases. In the meantime, get the space you intend for your studio prepared. If you don't have any jobs lined up by the time your equipment arrives, set up a still-life or grab a friend, and get some practice in.

Did you Like "Photography Lighting"?

Before you go, I'd like to say thank you so much for purchasing my book.

I know you could have picked from dozens of books on this subject, but you took a chance with mine, and I'm truly grateful for that.

So, once again, a big thanks for downloading this book and reading all the way to the end—I truly appreciate it.

Now I'd like to ask for a small favor if you don't mind:

Would you be so kind as to take a minute of your time and leave a review for this book on Amazon?

This feedback will help me continue to write the kind of books that help you get results. And if you loved it, then please feel free to let me know! :)

www.ingramcontent.com/pod-product-compliance
Lightning Source LLC
Chambersburg PA
CBHW071013180526
45168CB00003B/1405